My Tormented Soul

Tohon

ISBN   978-1-80369-567-9

www.newgeneration-publishing.com

 New Generation Publishing

By the same author:

- ➢ *Emil Joseph Burcik*
- ➢ *Life's Invisible Battles*
- ➢ *The Jihadi*
- ➢ *The Landscape of a Mind*

<u>In Memoriam</u>

Mourning those
Whom we lost
Before their time

Contents

Childhood

Prologue

The best part of my childhood was during 1955-60 when I was attending Dhaka Cantonment Primary School. My father was in the army, and we lived at the Kurmitola military compound. There was a parade ground sandwiched between the army barracks and the family quarters. Besides military parades, the ground had other useful purposes: a venue for sports and a variety of shows.

We lived next to the parade ground. Not only could we run and play there, but the open field offered an unrestricted view of the army barracks. We also enjoyed watching the military parades and marching band.

Even more exciting was the no-man's-land – we called it a jungle – bordering the old Dhaka–Chattogram railway line that ran past the cantonment. The jungle was full of bushes and trees. Our main attraction was the fruit trees, mostly guava, mango, and jackfruit. We also loved chasing the rabbits and aiming at birds with slingshots. So, beyond home and school, our happy, exciting days revolved around the parade ground and our adventures in the no-man's-land.

My World

Monsoon rains always brought me joy. I would lie idle on my bed and enjoy listening to the pounding *rim-jhim* on our tin-roofed house. I would also create music by covering and uncovering my ears with my palms in a fast, rhythmic cycle. I would watch through the window endless ripples in the vast expanse of shallow water on the inundated parade ground.

When the rain stopped – or sometimes even during the rain – we brothers would go out and run in the submerged grassland, but not without risking mother's reprimands.

I was curious in those days: Where does the rainwater fall from? After my initial struggle, I managed to crack the puzzle. The sky must be full of punched holes. Allah in heaven instructs the angels to turn on the water taps to allow water to drip down on the earth. There must be separate enclosed areas so that Allah can decide to send rain to some places while keeping it sunny in other areas. It made a lot of sense to me, and I was happy with my intellectual feat.

But then I also had a deeper curiosity: Do I have free will? I was sure that I did. So, I must find proof to establish it once and for all. Occasionally, I would run thought experiments – I do not remember the details – but was disappointed that none of the experiments proved for certain that I possessed free will.

Then one day, while we few friends were venturing in the jungle, we came across a guava tree full of fruits. We did not waste time. Like monkcys, we climbed up the branches and spread out looking for ripe, ready-to-eat guava. I caught sight of an unusually large, perfectly ripe fruit towards the end of a branch. Getting to it would be risky – a fear of falling to the ground assailed me, but the promise of the reward was stronger. I managed to reach the fruit, grabbed it, and then quickly came down to the ground to savour it.

A thought flashed through my mind. I gathered my strength and threw the guava away into the bush as far as I could.

I was thrilled with my success. I had finally proved my deeply held belief – I do possess free will – correct. But then I regretted my action. *I am stupid*, I thought. I had lost my hard-earned guava for nothing. How could I be sure that I was not fated to believe in free will and run experiments to prove myself right? How could I know that Allah was not driving my life, just as He decided when and where it would rain?

While my innate curiosity remained unresolved, I was successful in shaping my world in a different way.

There was a lanky, stray dog in our neighbourhood. Occasionally I would offer him leftover food. In return, he started guarding our door and wagging his tail as an expression of his gratitude.

While the monsoon season brought me joy, the dog's plight troubled me. Soaked in rainwater, shivering with cold, he would take shelter beneath the leafy banyan tree behind our house. Some evenings I would sneak the dog in and allow him to rest in the dark corner of our veranda, but not without my intrinsic feelings of guilt for the deceit.

It has been an age-old belief that, unlike cats, dogs are unclean animals and therefore not allowed inside a household. It bothered me as to why an innocent, faithful animal was considered unclean.

My mother's family came from Bikrampur (presently Munshiganj). It was (and still is) a historic region in Bengal with more than 2,500 years of Hindu antiquity and early Buddhist scholarship during the Emperor Ashoka's period (269 BC to 232 BC). One can still see the remnants of ancient Hindu and Buddhist temples in the area.

During holiday seasons we used to visit our maternal uncle, Hashem *mama*, and his family residing in the *nana*'s old house. I remember one particular occasion when Hashem *mama* took us to the Durga *puja mela*. There was a variety of shops. One particular shop was selling handmade pottery: coloured decorative pieces and vases; pots and pitchers; statues of Maa Kali, Ganesh, and the Buddha; and toys of all kinds, including dolls and miniature animal figures: tigers, elephants, crocodiles, and even cobras. I stood there motionless, looking at the clay art and sculptures. And then in a lightning flash, I saw the heavenly light shining on earth.

Allah in heaven must have first created men and animals in different shapes and forms and then, like filling empty pots and pitchers with water, He poured life into them all before placing them on earth. So, the dog and I must share the same life. Why would only one of us be "unclean" or even "inferior"?

When we got back home, in no time the dog and I became friends. I would call him Tommy. At my request, my mother allowed him to use our veranda as his refuge during the hot summer days, the rainy season, and cold evenings. Unfortunately, before his time, Tommy fell ill. For the first time, we carried him inside the house so that we could closely monitor his health. Tommy died shortly thereafter.

The dog went from being "unclean" to becoming a member of our family. We took some comfort in being able to care for him during his last days and grieved his passing.

I realised that the lanky, stray dog came to me not only as a friend, but also as a messenger from heaven.

Epilogue

More than sixty years have passed since that

momentous revelation. My life's pleasures have now been reduced to leisurely walks in the neighbourhood park, holding my grandson Himaloy's little, warm hand. His curious mind beholds the wondrous world around him. He asks me about the flying birds, falling rain, and endless other things. I reminiscence about my childhood world and share it with him.

A Long Walk

In June 1964, Nelson Mandela, along with several African National Congress leaders, was convicted in a court of law. The judge sentenced them all to life imprisonment. Surprisingly, it was a joyous occasion for Mandela and his fellow mates. They all shouted, "Hurray, we have a life to live!" In Mandela's own words: *I was prepared for the death penalty. To be truly prepared for something, one must actually expect it.*

As we now know, Mandela spent the first eighteen of twenty-seven years in jail at the brutal Robben Island. Subsequently he was moved to Pollsmoor Prison in Cape Town and then to Victor Verster Prison near Paarl. Finally, on 11 February 1990, Mandela walked out free.

In his autobiography *Long Walk to Freedom*, Mandela narrates that before his release, a colonel visited him in his cell and asked, '*Mandela, would you like to see the city?*'

"*I was not exactly certain what he had in mind, but I thought there was no harm in saying yes.*

"*We drove into Cape Town along the lovely road that runs parallel to the coast. He had no destination in mind, and we simply meandered around the city in a leisurely fashion. It was absolutely riveting to watch the simple activities of people out in the world: old men sitting in the sun, women doing their shopping, people walking their dogs. It is precisely those mundane activities of daily life that one misses most in prison. I felt like a curious tourist in a strange and remarkable land."*

I read *Long Walk to Freedom* back in 2000. Mandela's story in the Robben Island invoked my sentiments. In one hand, I was saddened for his inner turmoil, sense of despair, pain and suffering and, on the other hand, I asked myself, *Do I ever walk to a tree, even in my yard, to look at the beauty of a flower, let alone a leaf? Do I ever appreciate my freedom to walk, see, listen, and be close to nature?*

It became my ritual to walk routinely – short walks during the workdays and then long walks on weekends. More importantly, I began to enjoy my walks for they brought me peace and serenity.

In 2016 I took retirement. By then, our three boys had finished their university and taken up jobs. Two of them even got married, and then they all moved out to live independently. After selling our home, my wife and I moved to a two-bedroom apartment. While she continued with her academic career, I happily settled into my new life.

Now that I have time, I walk daily either on the walking trails, in the parks or on the roof top of our apartment (due to Covid lockdown), and on rainy days, I pace back and forth in the living room and even on the narrow balcony. During these walks in light of Mandela's life story, I begin to contemplate on many things.

I think of my mother who was bedridden during the last years of her life. I think of one of my friends who became immobile after he had suffered a stroke. And then there are others who have difficulties walking due to their poor health. I have come to believe that if I someday become immobile, I would have no regrets, for over the last two decades I already have not only walked to my heart's content but, at the same time, thought of suffering souls – men, women and children – around the globe. The saddened thoughts make me realise how fortunate I am to be able to lead a normal, happy life.

One of the kids I think of most is Ananda. He is a crippled teenage son of a friend of mine. Ananda is immobile and stays at home in his bed or a wheelchair. Although physically incapacitated, his mind has always been active, like any normal kid.

I feel sorry for Ananda and visit him whenever circumstances permit. While the family members engage themselves enjoying each other's company, I sit by Ananda in his lonesome room, holding his small, thin hand. He glances at me and smiles. His smile brings me shame for my occasional displeasure over life's mundane things.

I find it difficult to continue my conversation because I do not know how Ananda thinks; how his mind works. Sometimes I crack a joke, and he laughs. It helps me break the ice between us, even though we two live in vastly different worlds.

I have been curious and wanting to venture into the inner sanctum of his mind. So, I ask him what he loves most. He says, 'I enjoy it when *Ammu* takes me to the parkland. I love watching the kids in the playground. They all look so very happy and joyful.'

I keep probing, 'What would you do if God gave you one day of normal life?'

There is a moment of silence. Ananda is probably taken aback, but then he responds pensively, '*Chacha*, I would go out for a walk – a long walk. I would walk in the park, on the grass, by the river, on the rocky hills, sandy deserts, anywhere. I would walk, walk, and walk all day. The day would be like eternity in heaven.'

His words touch me deeply. I am overwhelmed. I look at his eyes and keep looking at him. He says, 'What?'

I say, 'That's a wonderful idea, Ananda. The best idea I ever heard of.'

Ananda's eyes brighten as he smiles at me. Deep down in my heart I cry, '*God, I am prepared to swap my life for his!*'

Postscript

The other day I received a phone call from Ananda's mother. She sobbed and said that their beloved son passed away last week due to health complications. She then pleaded, 'Please pray for his soul.'

Tears roll down my cheeks. All I know is that I love Ananda dearly and long to see him again in another world, under different circumstances.

Ananda and I, hand in hand, would set out for a long walk in the gardens of Eden. We would walk in the park, on the grass, by the river, on the rocky hills, sandy deserts and whatever comes to pass.

Defeat

Prologue

Life is a battlefield. Every living species fights a different battle; therefore, I can only talk about mine.

There are two battles that I have been fighting all my life: outer and inner. I am successful in my outer battle but the inner battles leave me wounded and defeated.

Outer Battle

I was lucky to be born into a family where my parents could offer the basic necessities of life. In addition, I was blessed with three distinctions: discipline, diligence and motivation. My fate took me – first to what was then West Pakistan (1966-73) where I did my college and university and then to the USA (1977-82) where I earned an MS and PhD in engineering.

My degrees offered me opportunities to work in the Middle East, Australia, the UK and South East Asia. Also, I have been happily married and blessed with three children and now two grandchildren.

Metaphorically, my life has been a mango seed in the hands of a farmer who sowed it in fertile soil. When the seed sprouted, he watered it and protected it from the grazing cattle. In time, the tree provided shade to his cattle, allowed birds to nest and hosted blossoms with fragrant flowers for bees to suck honey. Finally, it produced scented, sweet mangoes for men, monkeys, crows, flies and even nocturnal bats to enjoy.

Inner Battles

While I have been born with positive traits, I have also always been a sensitive, sentimental and emotional man. But my serious limitations have been timidity, poor reflexes and ineptitude in handling tools. So, I ended up being an introverted passive thinker as opposed to being proactive and assertive man.

Leadership is a quality I have lacked. I do not regret this, for it offered me the opportunity to spend time with my kids – to read them books, play with them, take them to parks and drive them to after-hour school activities. It also gave me time to keep my journal up to date and, as my childhood habit, attend to household chores, raking dry leaves and gardening. I would go running with our dog, Spotty, give him bath weekly and routinely clean up his poop from the backyard. While I failed to move up the ladder at work, I became a devoted family man.

But then every height has its depth. In my inner world I would endure agonies witnessing injustice and cruelty on this planet. The hate, anger and jealousy that I possess pained me too. The following episodes are excerpts from my journal to reflect on my inner torments.

Cowardice, Dhaka 1960
I am in Grade 4 at the Cantonment primary school. I watch silently as my classmate Abul Bashar is bullied by a couple of other boys. I do not have the courage to stand up for him.

It hurts me today just as it hurt me then. This episode remains one of the most shameful regrets of my life.

Famine, Sudan 1998
There is a serious famine in Sudan. The photographs of skeletal children with their out-of-proportion heads and bulging eyes are too painful to bear. Through their pain, I see my selfishness. Through their suffering, I begin to suffer.

Destruction, Brisbane 2001
As I water a lone sugar cane that I planted a while ago, I realise that it is foolish to consider oneself non-violent on the basis of becoming a vegetarian. I ask myself: Do the ants that I stamp on or drown suffer the same pain that humans endure when they are crushed under tons of rubble or swept away by a tidal bore? I know they do, for I see them running for their lives.

Even if one lives on vegetables, fruits and nuts, God knows how many lives are destroyed as lands are ploughed, plants are watered and crops are harvested.

I begin to see that living is rooted in violence, for life is sustained by life.

Violence, Brisbane 2001

It is cold morning. I step onto the lawn to get some sun. The plants, leaves and flowers, wearing dazzling dew, gently waving in the soft breeze, look beautiful. Then it occurs to me that I am blocking the sun, a vital source of their nourishment. So, I move aside. But it is not enough. I am still blocking the sun, this time from the grass. And worse, I am crushing it under my feet. I return to the driveway, under the shade of trees. I prefer plants to block the sun from me, rather than I should block it from them.

Cruelty, Washington DC 2017

Sadly, the American Constitution *does not* mention animals. While most religions consider animals inferior to humans, some even make it a ritual to slaughter cattle to appease God with gushing blood.

Life, including that of a tree, is sacred. There is no difference between living species when it comes to a mother's love for her offspring. One can never claim that a human mother cares for her kids more than a sow does for her piglets. Nor can one ever claim that a man loves his life more than an ant or even a plant loves its own.

<u>Killing Ground, World 2022</u>
While the world struggles to cope with Covid-19, the New Year begins with the Ukraine invasion. The world news no longer focuses on the bleeding wounds of Iraq and Afghanistan. The ongoing casualties in Syria and Yemen have become the norm, while it is needless to mention the endless Palestinian saga.

Since Cain killed his brother Abel the Earth has increasingly become a killing ground. Man now has the capability to destroy the world many times over. Beyond the age-old bayonets, bullets and bombs, there is now a new paradigm in modern warfare: 'Gitmo', 'WMD', 'drone attack' and 'collateral damage' – meaning 'no innocent blood on my hands'.

Epilogue

As I reflect on my life, I realise that my instincts, impulses, and emotion control my reactions. On one hand, I suffer for the suffering world and, on the other hand, I suffer for my weaknesses. So, I ask myself: how do I know that the life on this earth is not another world's hell? Or, perhaps, at the beginning of time, an all-powerful Author writes an epic masterpiece. Once the writing is done, He brings the story to life such that all the fictional characters become real. I am one of countless fictional characters playing a scripted role and, my wound, my pain and my defeat are all part of that eternal, epic masterpiece.

Or, maybe, in the beginning, the omnipotent God, creates a seed – call it the 'primal seed'. He infuses it with life's essential ingredients: instructions, knowledge, code, memory and, above all, adaptability. In time the seed evolves and diversifies within earth's varied environment, giving rise to diverse species – plants, land and aquatic animals, birds, insects and humans.

Therefore, human knowledge and wisdom, actions and reactions, joy and suffering, victory and defeat are nothing but fruit, like fruit in the trees – some are sweet, some are sour, some are bitter and some are even poisonous. But they all offer, in different ways, nourishment to the living world.

In that sense, Einstein's scientific achievement, Tagore's literary brilliance, Gandhi's non-violence and Hitler's brutality are all to do with the seeds they were born of. Like a river, life runs its course and all living species, big and small, beautiful and ugly and loving and fearsome are essentially equal. It all boils down to the primal seed God created in His infinite wisdom.

It is quite possible that my perceptions are nothing but fantasy. I am born confined within an eternal prison cell made up of mirrors such that the world around me is nothing but my own reflection in various shapes and forms.

Postscript

My long-time friend takes interest in my philosophical monologues, but never fully buys into them. Instead, he keeps probing my ideas. During a recent conversation he pointedly asked me, 'Do you have proof of your philosophical concepts?'

'No, I don't,' I reply.

'Then why would anyone buy it?'

'I'm not selling anything to anyone. I'm simply sharing my thoughts with you.'

'Thank you, but you must have some rationale behind your convictions.'

'Sorry, I have none. On the contrary, they all might well be total nonsense.'

'Then why do you hold onto them so passionately?'

'Like an ointment, it soothes my torments. It overcomes my inner pain. It brings solace to my soul.'

'In that case, please reveal the nature of your torments. It would help me appreciate your philosophical assumptions.'

'Indeed. Maybe the reason I fail to understand Buddhism is because I have no clue about the nature of the pain that drove Prince Gautama Siddhartha to forsake his family without an adieu, knowing that it would cause his parents, wife and son, and subjects deep pain and lasting resentment.'

'I suggest you start all over again. First, reveal the nature of your torment. Your philosophy will then be self-explanatory.'

A pause and a sigh. 'No. There is no point. Inner suffering has been a part of my life, all my life. I don't know how to explain it. Krishna Chandra Majumder, the 19th-century Bengali poet and writer, explains it better: চিরসুখীজন ভ্রমে কি কখন ব্যথিতবেদন বুঝিতে পারে? কী যাতনা বিষে, বুঝিবে সে কিসে কভূ আশীবিষে দংশেনি যারে? – meaning: How do I make someone feel the pain of venom when he has never been bitten by a deadly snake?'

'In that case, your philosophical world will remain inaccessible to me.'

'Probably.'

'I better not waste your time probing you on your thoughts, for you are a lonesome man in a world of your own.'

Quest for Truth

Prologue

During our childhood in Dhaka, my elder brother, Babul, and I went to a *moulvi* for the Qur'anic lessons. Within a year, we had learnt the recitation and memorised relevant *surah*s to perform *namaz*.

In school I was good at mathematics and science subjects. After college I went on to study engineering and in 1973 graduated from the Engineering University at Lahore. Religion did not come into play for me in those days – but then, at some point, it did, unexpectedly, and in an unusual way.

It was December 1979. I was attending the University of Texas at Austin, pursuing my PhD. One Sunday afternoon, the phone rang. The caller introduced herself as Sheila Stanley and she was phoning me regarding my published letter in *Time* magazine.

Sheila was a UT sophomore business student, a devout Christian and always happy with 'whatever Jesus wills'. We met occasionally during lunch breaks. At some point, she invited me to her church, Hope Chapel, to meet the pastor and founder, Daniel Davis. Meeting Dan was a turning point in my life.

Our first meeting took place in a country club where Dan ran his weekly worships. I found him to be deeply religious, a persuasive speaker and preacher who captivated his audience. We soon became friends and I even began to attend his Sunday services. If Professor Burcik[1] changed my outer life, Dan was a catalyst to transforming my inner world.

Dan would invite me to his house for dinner and occasionally take me out to lunch. He mostly talked about Jesus. I realised that he had only good intentions and wanted me to accept Jesus as my saviour. He gave me a copy of the Bible and asked me to study it. I said I would and I did. While I appreciated his friendship and generosity, to his disappointment, I begged to differ with him on religious grounds.

One day Dan asked me, 'Okay, Mohammad, I know about the five pillars of Islam, but I've never read the Qur'an. Please tell me, what does it say?'

His question put me in an awkward position, for I had learnt to recite the Qur'an in Arabic without understanding its meaning. I resolved to do something about this hole in my religious knowledge and embarked on what would become a life-long quest.

---

[1] Tohon, *Emil Joseph Burcik*, New Generation Publishing, London, 2021

The Quest

I bought a copy of the English version of the Qur'an and began my quest. I understood God's revelations, His message and the warning to His creation. Unfortunately, I found nothing new from my first read, but I felt that I must have missed something. I had read the life and times of Abu Yazid al-Bestami, a distinguished Muslim Sufi, and admired him greatly. I asked myself: what did Sufi Yazid find in the Qur'an that made him a godly man?

I will return to this episode later, for I want to share other developments that were shaping my life at that time.

I took an interest in physics and had been reading books on science, particularly the works of Isaac Asimov. I was also reading Albert Einstein's life stories and learnt that he had three framed photos hanging in his home in New Jersey, where he was a distinguished professor at Princeton University from 1933 until his death in 1955. One of the photos was of Mahatma Gandhi. It struck me: what would a celebrated physicist like Einstein have to do with Gandhi?

I acquired a copy of Louis Fischer's *The Life of Mahatma Gandhi*. I could not stop as I turned the pages. What I read brought me shame, for I had not read about Gandhi before. I went on to buy several more books on Gandhi. In his autobiography, *My Experiments with Truth*, Gandhi wrote that it was the *Bhagavad-Gita* that had shaped his life.

I bought a copy of the *Gita* and read it almost non-stop. I found it one of the most captivating books I had ever read. Over the years I went on to study *The Upanishads, The Vedas, The Ramayana* and *The Mahabharata*. I even read several books on Swami Ramakrishna – the most engrossing life story I have ever read. I was enthralled to have discovered such a rich trove of philosophy and religious beliefs in my backyard. I realised that my attraction to Indian philosophy was probably due in part to my genetic inheritance, for I am descended from Hindu ancestors. But then I was also attracted to Greek philosophy and influenced by Socratic thought, and I do not know how I could have been related to the Greeks! Next, I read about the Popes, the Vatican and Catholicism. I was also fascinated by the life and times of Adolf Hitler. Over the years I have studied him more than any other person, including Mahatma Gandhi, the Buddha and Nelson Mandela. Does Hitler's blood run in my veins?

At some point, I came across Richard Dawkins' books on genes. I found them most intriguing, for they offered a scientific explanation of life. In his book *The Ancestor's Tale: A Pilgrimage to the Dawn of Life,*

Dawkins sums it up beautifully: "Humans as a species, as well as humans as individuals, are temporary vessels containing a mix of genes from different sources. Individuals are temporary meeting points on the crisscrossing routes that genes take through history."

As I understood it, genes not only contribute to life's building blocks, but they also pass forward information, knowledge and even traits from ancestors to their descendants. Each gene is a little window back into the past. I would not be surprised if I turn out to be a mixed bag of genes sourced from the Hindus, Greeks, Muslims, Jews, Catholics, Hitler, Shakyamuni, the Pharaohs, Africans, chimpanzees and apes, ants and wasps, and plants and trees – our original ancestors. Plants feed us, nurture us and even sustain the environment. Without them, the living world would not only become orphaned, but die as if deprived of its mother's milk.

By 1982, I was happily married and had finished my PhD. We moved to Dhahran to take up my new job and stayed there for the next five years.

Time in Dhahran was fruitful in many ways. Firstly, I became involved with Save the Children projects in Bangladesh and supported many of their programs: sponsoring malnourished children, renovation of flood-damaged schools and setting up scholarship funds for disadvantaged, meritorious students. During my yearly visits to Bangladesh, the Save the Children officials would take me to the project sites to show the work progress first hand. Secondly, we visited Mecca and Medina on several occasions and, thirdly, I took time to reread the Qur'an. By then I had also read the lives of many Sufis including – Al-Junaid Abo 'l-Qusem, Rabe'a Basri and Mansur Al-Hallaj. Once again, I asked myself: what did these men / women find in the Qur'an that inspired them to become men / women of God?

I wish to clarify that I never thought even for a moment that spirituality was something unique to Islam, for I knew that there had been spiritual men and women in other religions. As Sri Ramakrishna says, "There are many paths to scale a mountain peak."

The other factor that shaped my life is that during my high school days at Chattogram, we grew up among Hindu, Muslim, Christian and Buddhist schoolmates and neighbourhood friends. We loved all the religious holidays and festivals: Ramadan, Eid, Durga Puja, Buddha Purnima, Christmas, to name a few. Many of our teachers were Hindus wearing *dhoti*. As a mark of respect and custom, we would bow down and touch their feet (*kodombuchi*) as we would do to other teachers, parents and elderly relatives. Words like heaven and hell, believer and infidel, glory and sin had no place in my childhood innocence. They have no place even now.

In late 1987, we immigrated to Australia. After living there for three years, we travelled to the Sultanate of Oman and then moved back to Australia in 1995. By then we were a family of six, including our dog, Spotty. While keeping busy with the family and jobs, I kept searching for and studying as many sources of wisdom, philosophy and science as I could.

Seek, and ye shall find – Matthew 7:7. It was Karen Armstrong's books, *A History of God, Islam – A Short Story* and *Muhammad – A Prophet for our Time* that opened my inner eye. This time I had glimpses of light and could relate to the verses in the Qur'an that must have inspired men and women to reach nearer to God.

One of the most profound words in Islam is 'Islam' itself, meaning submission – submission to the will of God. There are two other equally profound words: 'Qur'an', meaning recitation, and *'masjid'*, meaning place for prostration. 'Submission', 'recitation' and 'prostration' became my guiding stars.

I do not claim that I understood the Qur'an in its full dimensions and depth. It may take a man one lifetime, several lifetimes or even infinite lifetimes before he comprehends God's revelations. I also come to believe that it is not only the Abrahamic Scriptures, but Scriptures of all religions and faiths are

God's revelations. And, that music and arts, literature and philosophy, science and mathematics too are God's revelations. There is nothing in the universe that is not His revelation. I love watching Sir David Attenborough's documentaries on the wondrous living world. To me it is a revelation in its most sublime form.

How does an ant do what it does? How does a weaver bird (*babui phakhi*) build a well-knitted nest? How does a chameleon change its colour? How does a caterpillar transform itself to a butterfly? How does a seed transform itself into roots, shoots, branches and leaves, then blossoming flowers and eventually into sweet fruits? How does a plant know which colour, fragrance and taste will attract the bees? My inner eye sees God's invisible hands everywhere and in everything, including life's evolutionary process, the movement of the heavenly bodies and, above all, the universal laws that govern the cosmos and beyond.

From 2005 up until my retirement in 2016, I worked in consulting, university teaching and professional training. My job required travelling within and outside Australia: the UK, the USA, the Middle East and South East Asia. Yet I was never distracted from my quest. I would submerge myself in spiritual thoughts and meditations, and I continued to pen my innermost thoughts. I committed to memory verses not only from the Qur'an, but also from the Bible and the Hindu and Buddhist Scriptures. I even memorised Tagore's spiritual poems. I could freely move from one to the other without any issue.

Dreams are a strange and unexplained phenomenon. During my lifetime, I have had many unusual dreams about visiting places, meeting people and souls, repeated dreams and dreams within dreams. I even once had an after-death experience. On two occasions I have been in the company of the Prophet Muhammad (peace be upon him) and once met Jesus Christ (*pbuh*) in another dream. When I confided to my mother about having met the Seal of the Prophets (*pbuh*), she revealed that my father had once confided to her a similar dream. My religious fervour must have been passed down to me by my father.

Since my retirement, I go out for daily walks and, among other things, I recite verses from memory as if they were my passionate songs. As I look back, I see that my life has been in God's hands all along, every moment of it. I believe that there are only two things that exist: God and His will. His will prevails universally and eternally such that past, present and future all coexist. Life on this earth is nothing but a foregone future and there is no conflict between the Creator and His creation.

A question arises, though: why is there injustice and violence, torture and execution, poverty and starvation, sickness and death?

I have no clue. I am chained by five senses and locked in a four-dimensional space-time domain. On the contrary, I believe God possesses countless senses and countless dimensions. How on earth, then, a captive little creature would ever know Him or comprehend His mind and His work?

Do I know myself? No, I don't. How would I then know my fellow men, let alone the Creator and His universe? All I know is that He exists everywhere and in everything, including every gene in every living body. God is life and life is God, regardless of whose life it is: man and woman, ant and elephant, cockroach and termite, plants and fungi, or anything else. He is formless and yet appears in innumerable forms. Metaphorically, if life is water, then the living bodies are pots, pans and pitchers of different shapes, sizes and colours. No man is beneath another man and no living species is beneath another living species, including Homo sapiens.

Such thoughts may appear as figures of a blind man's wild imagination, but if my thoughts flow from God, then they are His revelations. If someone disagrees with me, his thoughts too are His revelations. Why would God send conflicting messages? To me, they are like interlocking pieces with opposite interfaces that fit into a cosmic jigsaw puzzle. Everything in this universe including right and wrong, good and evil, holy and unholy are nothing but jigsaw pieces.

A termite's life might be inconsequential in the cosmic play, but the cosmos would be incomplete without it, just as a jigsaw puzzle is incomplete without a missing piece, no matter how small. And, like light and shadow, height and depth, and particle and anti-particle, right and wrong, good and evil, virtue and vice go hand in hand. They are not only intertwined, but also sustain each other. If my thinking is correct, then the cosmic play might as well be a zero-sum game, meaning, at any given moment, the sum total of cosmic energy is zero.

My thoughts are fruits on a tree that stem from a unique combination of *active* genes inherited from predecessors all the way back to origin. There are trillions of genes in a single human body, including good and bad genes, kind and brutal genes, honest and cheating genes, love and hate genes, free will and fated genes, and 'God' and infidel genes. The genetic 'make-up' for every human, or every living species for that matter, is unique just as it is unique for every tree or their variants. A man's strength and vulnerability, vice and virtue, emotion and passion, and, above all, personality as to who he is, are dictated by the *active* genes or his make-up. The Himalaya can be moved but not a man's nature for its root is way too deep. Paulo Coelho rightly says, "You do not choose your life, it chooses you."

Like a tree, I too am born of a seed with information, knowledge and traits. I have my senses with which I observe nature and study books and scriptures, but they only help me to reconnect to and recollect from a pre-existing knowledge that flows from a supreme Being whom I call God. Dawkins calls it a *Watchmaker*[2] – an unconscious, blind Watchmaker, without foresight. I think the opposite. Yet, we both are correct because that is the way the opposing perceptions fit into the cosmic jigsaw puzzle and thereby contribute to the eternal zero-sum game.

When I shared my thoughts with my friend, he listened to me patiently. When I had finished, he asked, 'Is this the "ultimate truth"?'

I replied, 'No, I do not believe that a captive man can ever make truth certain and, therefore, "ultimate".'

My friend went on the offensive, 'Yet you expect others to see the world the way you do, ignoring the fact that, like a lost traveller in a desert, your quest might have led you to a mirage, in which you are unable to distinguish between the real and illusory nature of your senses.

'Maybe you should adapt and look at the world the way others see it. After all, like yours, their world views too are fruits on trees that stem from their unique make-up.

---

[2] Richard Dawkins, *The Blind Watchmaker,* Penguin Books, 1988

Do not fruit from different trees have differing colours, fragrances, and tastes?

'Or maybe you should consider a more simplistic view: like yourself, others too are characters on the cosmic stage playing their scripted roles.'

My friend continued, 'And then you say there are only two things that exist: God and His will. Maybe you are wrong on that precept. The two things are not God and His will but yourself and your invisible mirror. The world you see is nothing but your own reflections in different shapes and forms.'

'And lastly', my friend went on, 'You're merely a grain of sand at the foothills of the Himalayas. It is time you bow to the Everest.'

'Indeed,' I said. 'I'm enlightened to see myself through your eyes, my friend. Yes, it is time I bow to the mount and, also take a vow never to speak again.'

'I do not think that's a good idea, my friend. Your silence would mean your thoughts would die with you.'

'What good are they to anyone anyway? Every pain is unique and every suffering soul has to find a balm that would befit him.'

Epilogue

It is August 2022. Sheila Stanley (now Sheila Vance) and I continue to correspond to this day. Over the years, Daniel Davis, the pastor, and I have continued to exchange our views on faith. In 2009, I visited Houston to meet Sheila and her family. In 2011, I travelled to Austin to meet Dan and his wife, Joann. These reunions were joyous occasions for us all. I was happy to find that Sheila and Dan continued to live happily by their deeply held belief: "Whatever Jesus wills".

I am blessed to have lived a fruitful life, although not without inner torments. It has offered me the opportunity to travel to distant lands, meet diverse people and dedicate myself to a spiritual quest.

I am now biding my time, for I am already seventy-two years old. My parents and my eldest and youngest brothers have all passed away between the ages of sixty-five and seventy-two. My only surviving sibling, with whom I attended the *moulvi*, is currently in precarious condition.

I do think of death. Will the passage be painful? But then, isn't life on this earth a foregone future? Am I not a spectator watching my own life unfold? Why do I worry? Yet I cannot ignore it because, during the course of my life, I have endured agonising ordeals.

Masud
On a hot summer day, during my days in Lahore, I lost my roommate, Masud. He was twenty-two. As part of his final year of study, he was constructing a prototype solid-fuel rocket. After long, hard work, his rocket was

ready for its first test on 13 June 1972. One moment Masud was full of life and the next moment he was gone – gone for ever. During the very first test something went horribly wrong. The blast took away his life.

Anis

During my Dhaka visits, I would occasionally meet my Lahorian friend, Anis. He was Masud's old friend from their days at Faujdarhat Cadet College, Chattogram. They both were academically outstanding. Anis shared with me his sad story.

On 20 May 1987 (22 Ramadan), Anis lost his younger son, Munmu. He was eight years old and healthy but died within a matter of hours after he was struck by a rare illness.

The unexpected tragic loss was catastrophic for him and his family. Yet while they were still reeling from this tragedy, on 20 August 1997, their other son, Maruf, a third-year engineering student, aged twenty-one, drowned in Cox's Bazar beach along with three of his classmates who were trying to rescue him. Maruf's body was recovered but, despite a search by the naval ships, the other three boys were lost in the sea for ever.

I spent hours with Anis in coffee shops, but failed to fully comprehend his inner pain. It was too deep. His heart problem got worse. He closed down his business and stayed home in the company of his wife, Zubaida, and daughter, Mouri, a talented architect.

During our last meeting, with tears in his eyes, Anis said that he had accepted his losses as God's will and made peace with His decisions.

Baset and Quazi
During 2005-6 I was working in North Wales, England. On Friday, 30 December 2005, Babul phoned me from Dhaka while watching breaking news on the TV.

Two PetroBangla officials and their wives had been burnt to death in a tragic road accident. Their charred bodies were beyond recognition.

One of the officials, Senior General Manager Baset, happened to be my classmate from the Lahore days. The other official, Quazi, Director of Planning and Director General of the Bangladesh Petroleum Institute, was my former colleague at the Titas Gas Field. The shocking news came to me out of the blue and overwhelmed me.

Quazi and I had worked together at the gas field during 1976. Since then, I had met him only once – sometime in the mid-nineties. I never met his family. From our brief association I knew him as a modest person and a perfect gentleman.

I first met Baset back in September 1968 at the Engineering University, Lahore. By early 1973 we both graduated with petroleum engineering degrees. Upon returning to Dhaka in late 1973 we were both busy looking for jobs. First, we worked in a gas pipeline construction company for a year and then joined PetroBangla in early 1975. We got separated in mid-1977 when I got an opportunity to go to the US for higher studies.

While doing my PhD I came to Dhaka for a visit during the 1981 New Year's break and got married and so did Baset later in the year.

During my subsequent visits, I would look forward to seeing Baset. He would take a day off and we would go out to catch up. First, we would spend time in a roadside café drinking hot chai and eating samosa, *rosgolla* and *chamcham*. We would mostly reminiscence about our good old Lahore days. We would then walk aimlessly along the roads, alleys and in the parks. After lunch we would indulge ourselves in smoking, buying loose cigarettes from a *pan-dokan*. We would shake hands before dusk and not see each for a few years.

During our family visit to Dhaka in December 2003, I took my wife and three boys to visit Baset and his family at their Bailey Road apartment. By then he also had three kids: two sons and a daughter.

After the accident I was desperate to find out more: what had happened, how had it happened and, more importantly, how were their families coping with the tragedy? During my subsequent trips to Dhaka, I enquired with some friends about Baset and Quazi but failed to make a headway.

It was not until last month (July 2022) that Murshed, a long-forgotten colleague from the gas field days, contacted me, unexpectedly. He said that he had bumped into one of our common colleagues, Mansur, at a pharmacy and learnt about my whereabouts. I thought Murshed might have some information and, in fact, he did. He turned out to be a God-sent messenger.

Murshed managed to track down Quazi's son and daughter (Amit and Sumaya) and Baset's eldest son and his daughter (Nabid and Nafisa). With their permission he forwarded me their contact details. Amit and Sumaya did not know me. After two long decades and their lives turned upside down, Nabid and Nafisa would not remember me. Even I had forgotten their names and would not have recognised their faces.

I sent out emails to them all explaining who I was and why it had taken me seventeen long years to reach out to them. The flurry of emails and conversations that followed was an emotional journey for us all. When I first spoke to Nafisa on phone she said, '*Chacha*, why after so many years?' and sobbed. I barely managed my emotion.

I was able to establish a bond with them all and it blossomed. It was like the first rain on a dry, parched land after a long spell of drought. We all knew that we had a long journey ahead of us as we relived the events that had changed the course of our lives forever.

On the fateful day, Murshed, then a PetroBangla Director, along with several high officials, had been headed to attend a ceremony at the Sylhet Gas Field. There was a third minibus, about an hour behind, carrying Quazi, his wife (Nasrin) and their twenty-three-year-old son, Amit. Also riding with them were Baset, his wife (Mahfuja) and their nine-year-old son, Nahin. Quazi took the front seat with the driver. Baset, Mahfuja, and Nasrin sat in the middle row from left to right and Amit and Nahin occupied the back seats.

At around ten in the morning near Narsingdi, which ironically happened to be Baset's hometown, there was a thunder in the blue. It had to do with Mahfuja's frantic scream. Awakened from his doze, Amit saw his mom and dad turning their faces towards him. But the view of a speeding yellow truck that was about to hit them head on horrified him.

Amit was knocked unconscious upon impact. The bystanders managed to rescue Amit and Nahin before the gas-driven vehicle exploded into flames. The raging flames took five lives in a matter of minutes: Baset and Mahfuja, Quazi and Nasrin, and the driver.

Amit and Nahin were rushed some fifty kilometres to the Dhaka Pongu (Orthopaedic) Hospital. In due course, they both recovered from their injuries. Amit had to go through nineteen major surgeries over the next five years. Only God knows the agony, the torment and the pain the survivors went through. In addition to their physical injuries, their souls must have been ablaze in a raging hellfire ever since the traumatic event.

The shock, distress and devastation of the surviving children were beyond my comprehension. The painful events inflicted me with a deep wound and a shameful guilt. How would I ever face Baset? He must have been watching the subsequent unforgiving episode from heaven. And, to his utter disbelief, his good, old friend of forty years was of no help.

Yes, I was away in a distant land, but that does not ease my anguish. My friend consoled me by saying that I should not blame myself for what happens to others. But it does not work for me; it never did. I cannot even clear my conscience by saying it was all 'God's will'. Nor can I uphold my deeply held belief that we all live a life with a foregone future.

It is an irony that, at the end, my life-long quest wrecked me mercilessly. As my only recourse, I am willing to face a painful passage that might unburden my soul and free me from my guilt.

My Two Worlds

Now that I am old and have time,
I take stock of my life.
I crisscross as far back as my memory goes,
Along my chequered memory lane.

As I remember,
I have always been happy even without toys.
Happiness was my twin but, sadly,
Not without its dark shadow.

I would be saddened to see the suffering
among the living –
The animals, insects, men and even plants.
I cried during my lonely hours;
I gave away my precious possessions; and
I even became one with them, sharing their
pain.
And then I begged God again and again
For His mercy, but nothing changed.

All through my life
My happiness was burdened with sorrow.
It was like an ever-vigilant shadow of the
light;
It was like a deep, dark abyss of the height.
All through my life
I remained a prisoner in my own solitary,
dark cell.

Now, before I die, I want to break free from
the chains.
I searched for so long, so deep in my soul,
Only to hear a whisper again and again:
Thou shall know Truth and
Truth shall let you know that you are
chained.

Maybe I live in two worlds –
One of darkness and the other of light.
I am chained in one but free in the other;
I suffer in one but celebrate the other.
And when I die, I will be reborn in the other,
Without sorrow.

The Portraits

Prologue

Over a span of more than two decades (2000-22), I have received numerous responses from my readers. As I see it, their ruminations and reflections are lines and shades of sketches that eventually generated a portrait – a portrait of a man / writer / tormented soul. But then, as Elbert Hubbard says, "Man, like Deity, creates in his own image. When a painter paints a portrait, he makes two – one of himself and the other of the sitter."

The Painters and their Sketches

The following passages are the responses from my readers. Their names are arranged in alphabetical order without the chronological timeline.

Sadly, for varied reasons, some of the notes have been lost over time.

➢ <u>Ayesha Alam (Jishan)</u>
Dear Jishan,

I remember, you wrote me a note, a while ago, after reading *The Jihadi*. I am sorry, I have lost it. It always makes me feel joyous and sad at the same time when I get something precious. Sad – because of the fear of losing it.

I first met your *boro mama*, Masud, in Lahore back in September 1968. Fifty-four years have passed since then. While I cannot reach him, I am happy to be connected to his niece.

Mama

➢ <u>Michael Burcik</u>
Dear Mohammad,

I did get a chance to read your stories. I appreciate you sharing your personal reflections with me. In a way, when I read them, it is like you are once again sitting on our deck sharing them in person, just as you did it in 2014 with your story about my grandfather, Emil Burcik.

I am not sure what brought us together, but I am truly grateful that our paths have crossed. Our discussions and emails will become stories that I along with our two sons, Derek and Evan, will share for years to come. You are now a part of our lives.

My only regret is that our friendship is one that must extend thousands of miles. Still, I think there is a connection we have that is closer than those friends whom I see on a daily basis.

Please keep in touch. Hopefully, someday you can share more stories with us, in person.

Michael

➢ <u>William J Clinton</u>
Dear Mohammad,

Thank you very much for writing to me about my book *My Life* and for sharing a copy of your article "Magic Touch". I put a lot of time, effort, and thought into my memoirs, and it means a lot to me that you have taken a personal interest in my work. I deeply appreciate your words of support.

As I continue to do what I can do to help improve our world, I am grateful for the input and ideas of people like you.

Sincerely,

Bill Clinton

Dear Mohammad,

Thank you for sending me a copy of *Life's Invisible Battles*. Congratulations on sharing your story with the world. I look forward to reading it.

I appreciate your kind words, and I am sending you my best wishes.

Sincerely,

Bill Clinton

➢ <u>Daniel Davis</u>
Dear Mohammad,

I am in Nashville, Tennessee, right now, returning from the funeral of my brother. He died at the age of seventy-eight and he had a wonderful and active life right up to the time he died.

He and his wife had been out shopping.

They returned home. He was in his lounge chair, watching TV. From the kitchen, she heard him say, "Jesus, oh Jesus." She looked around and saw him with his arms raised. He then slumped over and died shortly thereafter.

Do you remember your visits to our church – Hope Chapel – when we used to meet at the Country Club back in 1980? The same brother came and stood in front of you and said some words. We call it prophecy. It seemed to disturb you and you never returned to our services thereafter. I have always been curious why it bothered you so much. I pray that God's favor and blessing is upon you and that you know His love and grace.

Your brother, Dan

Dear Mohammad,

Thank you for your words of comfort regarding my brother's death. His death had a special impact on me. He was a godly man who loved Jesus, my Lord, very dearly. I am the youngest of six children. Now only my sister and I remain. It feels as though I am the patriarch of the family.

Ours has been a family totally devoted to our love of Jesus and our conviction that we will be reunited with Him in the eternal life that follows. As I learn more about modern physics, the more I am convinced that science is moving beyond the thoughts of a universe as described by Newton – a universe that has many dimensions. I am convinced that a Being of profound dimension has ordered an existence that transcends our senses. Somehow, my brother and others that I have known (even me!) have been allowed to taste the joy of life that lies beyond.

My father, my mother, my three brothers, my sister and their spouses all have preceded me into that realm. Somehow, I see that realm holding all the intimations and unrealized hopes that God has placed in my heart. There I will know the deepest expressions of love, peace, adventure, joy, and thrill that I do not have the capacity to experience in this limited dimension that I now enjoy.

I believe that God has kept us connected over these many years for a purpose that goes beyond our understandings. I love you, my brother, and desire to be united with you again – either in this or life beyond.

Your brother, Dan

Dear Mohammad,

I remember our last email exchange, where I tried to outline my understanding of your world view as communicated in your published journal *The Landscape of a Mind*. As I recall it, what I wrote in the outline, my thoughts are that I did not do our friendship justice. Your book is a tremendous blessing to me, not because I am converted to your worldview, but because of the celebration of friendship that I see recorded. We have had some wonderful exchanges of thoughts over the years. It seems that God has provided us with the basis of respecting the honor and dignity of each other's views. I thank you so much for your commitment to our friendship.

Your brother, Dan

➤ <u>Turgay Ertekin</u>
Dear Mohammad,

I have just finished reading *Life's Invisible Battles*. It has been a wonderful treat for me to read it today as it was heart-warming in the late November cold weather in Central Pennsylvania. I was planning to read the book in a couple of days, but after I started reading it today, I could not put the book down, as your literary work is totally captivating. Thank you very much for sharing your inner world with your readers. From time to time, I found some parallels with my own thoughts, but your inner world is definitely much more exquisite.

Once again, congratulations on a job wonderfully done.

Turgay

Last weekend, I received from Amazon *Emil Joseph Burcik.* I enjoyed reading it and, once again, in one sitting. It brought back many wonderful and warm memories of Dr. Burcik, and I thank you for doing that. Once again, many thanks for warming up my daily life by sharing your memoirs.

Turgay

Thank you very much for your note and your most recent story, "Quest for Truth". As usual, I read this piece with excitement. It takes the reader to a twisted road where changes, difficulties, and happiness in our lives are met at each turn of the path set for us. Again, many thanks for sharing your story.

Turgay

➤ John Frisch
The Landscape of a Mind
This work is a multi-layered contemplative journal. One layer consists of the joys and tribulations of everyday life: family, friends, marriage, raising children, school, work, and paying the mortgage. Another layer consists of ruminations on whether we have free will or not, the dualities of life and the paradoxical nature of good and evil, virtue and vice, perpetrator and victim. Still another layer consists of philosophical and religious explorations, drawing both from eastern religious traditions and western physics – an exotic and eclectic mix. A favorite layer of mine is an exchange of

letters between two men born on the opposite sides of the globe, with worldviews as far apart as their origin. Yet the author and the Christian pastor each maintain their respect and friendship for one another while continuously talking past each other about their worldview. It is a fascinating exchange.

I found much to ponder and enjoy in this contemplative work.

John Frisch

The Jihadi
Jihad means struggle and this is a story of some of the struggles of a native of Bangladesh who fortuitously finds himself living a dream as a graduate student in the United States, with a professor who becomes both his mentor and friend. Alas, a stroke strikes the professor and the student struggles with the decline and passing of his "old man".

The trail soon leads to the rescue of a Texas cockroach, through the anonymous canyons of New York City, and on to Saudi Arabia, where he goes on to his pilgrimage to Mecca. His hajj quickly becomes a struggle to maintain his pure spiritual intent with the many frustrations of navigating the crowded rituals with his companions. Spiced with quotations from Muslim mystics his pilgrimage becomes an unforgettable story.

Later there are further struggles, grappling with the nature of sin, a spendthrift brother, the evidence for evolution, the pressures of work and family, unintended consequences, the rumor mill, and even whether man has a free will. A further and comical life and death struggle ensues when an uninvited guest, a snake, joins a dinner party at his home in Oman.

Years later, the author struggles with the reality of his youthful dreamland of America, his beacon of freedom, human dignity, human rights, and the rights of other nations becoming dimmed for him by events following 9/11. He concludes with a final struggle that touches on his heroes, Mahatma Gandhi and Nelson Mandela, in his article – "The Magic Touch" – and how they free him from his negative perception of an American President.

The Jihadi is an eclectic and enjoyable read for anyone who enjoys contemplating the many struggles of life.

John Frisch

Emil Joseph Burcik
How about that! Kindnesses passing from generation to generation in completely unpredictable ways. I sure love the story and the sequels.

Thanks again for sharing your literary efforts with me, Mohammad. It appears that you have turned what you consider your shortcomings into a strength. Even for one not as sensitive as you are, it is distressing to me to read the headlines of recent weeks.

Well, you have said before that your writing was finished, so I hope you are wrong that this is your final story. In the meantime, I hope you are able to enjoy lots of time with your grandsons.

John

I enjoyed reading "Quest for Truth". It is interesting that we seem to have followed parallel paths. I was raised a Catholic, but also studied with some Protestant Christians when I was in college, which altered my views in ways my parents did not necessarily appreciate. And every time I travelled to a new place, I have taken the time to learn something about their culture and religion.

In Oman, during my lunch break, I would read a chapter or two from an English translation of the Qur'an. It soon became obvious to me how similar the roots of Judaism, Christianity, and Islam really are.

I also enjoyed the Islamic holidays, and, luckily, some of my Omani friends invited me to join them. A very memorable moment happened when my mom visited me and we were invited to an Eid celebration. She never stopped talking about that for as long as she lived.

When I went trekking in Nepal, I visited the Buddhist and Hindu temples there and bought my first book on Buddhist teachings.

In Japan I visited the quite different Zen Buddhist shrines and also some Shinto shrines. In Taiwan I visited some of the Taoist and Confucian shrines. In recent years I have read some classic Jewish works (after a genetic ancestry test showed that I had a tiny bit of Jewish ancestry, seven or eight generations ago).

You got me to read Gandhi and Mandela, which I surely prefer to Stalin, Hitler, and Mao, but something makes me sample both the best and the worst of how humans treat one another. Of course, I have had an interest in scientific subjects of all kinds since I was doing science fair projects in elementary school. There are so many fascinating and marvellous things in the world of nature.

I like to take a walk with my camera and photograph plants, animals and insects I find along the way and then try to identify them when I get home and learn something about them. I call this my accidental naturalist studies. The universe is so vast, as shown in the Hubble photos, that humans will never get to see but the tiniest fraction of everything that exists.

I had to smile when you wrote, "Why would God send conflicting messages?" Yes, why indeed? It is a puzzle to me. I just try to pick up some wisdom from all the traditions. Whatever the full truth is, I don't ever expect to find out in this world.

Thank you again for sharing your thoughts with me and for your friendship.
John

➢ <u>Robert Fuglei</u>
Mohammad,

I enjoyed reading "My Childhood World" – the details are wonderfully rich and concrete and imagistic. There are some abstractions, but they are always rooted in detail.
Robert

➢ <u>Shoma Hasmat</u>
Dear Shoma,

I am sorry, I have lost your note. I did enjoy your company although I met you only a few times. You were so young and yet you fully understood my unorthodox philosophical concepts. I thank you for your interest.
Kabir uncle

➢ <u>Ismat Hossain</u>
Dear Kabir *bhai*,

I have had the great opportunity to read your book, *Life's Invisible Battles*. As I read it, I found that every story has its own path to nourish the reader.

I learnt about your journey through several aspects of your colourful life, which is still shining with new windows opening every day, and about how you became the special "Tohon".

I was amazed by your description of how blessed we are by having what we have. I had tears in my eyes while reading about the Milky Boy in your story "The Journey Back Home". It truly captured the realities of life.

The crippled boy's words in "A Long Walk", "I would go out for a walk. I would walk, walk and walk all day. The day would be like eternity in Heaven." I felt the deep truth inside these words. Very meaningful indeed!

"The waves, tides, moon, earth, sun, galaxy, universe.... how they are controlled by each other" and the Bubble description was absolutely stunning!

There is much more I can say about your writing, but it simply wouldn't do it justice, so I will finish by saying I am looking forward to what you write next!

Ismat

➢ Khondkar Islam (Munir)

Munir *bhai*,

I am sorry, I have lost your note. I remember, during one of my visits to Dhaka, you took me out to lunch. After the lunch you pulled out your notebook with your notes and queries on *The Landscape of a Mind*. We had a wonderful time together.

Tuhin

➢ John Keasberry

During my visit to Dr Kabir in Perth in 2009, I was impressed by his liberal view on religion, world affairs and family life. We became close friends then, soul-mates, if you like.

I was also impressed to learn that he was the author of two biographical memoirs, *The Landscape of a Mind* and *The Jihadi*, which explained and reflected the discussions we had have and will have in the future. Both the works are highly recommended and acclaimed, not only in general, but also on a personal level.

His quiet, understated disposition demands respect in communicating seemingly difficult subjects and present them in a such a way, that his readers understood them.

John Keasberry

> Mahbub Khandaker (Titan)
Dear Tuhin *bhaiya*,

Amidst all the doom and gloom of this pandemic situation, your letter brought a ray of hope and a sense of belonging. Congratulations! And thanks for sharing.

Thank you for sharing Daniel Davis' letter as well. Indeed, our lives are put together as a tapestry woven from encounters with friends at crossroads.

I look forward to the day when we can get together again and share bits and pieces of our experiences as we journey through life. Titan

➤ <u>Mahtab Kabir</u>

Hi *Abbu*,

I have been reading *Life's Invisible Battles* slowly, just a story or two before bed.

I have read most of the stories before, but I still very much enjoyed reading them again. I finished "Bolai" last night. The name Bolai is familiar to me, but I am not sure whether I had read this short story before. Either way, I enjoyed reading it.

I am familiar with the themes you explore: genetic inheritance, lack of free will (both from genetic inheritance as well as being at the mercy of cosmic forces beyond our comprehension— i.e., bubbles on the waves), but it is still nice to be able to see the same themes reinforced in different stories and approached from slightly different angles.

I think my most favourite story so far is "Masud - My Lost Friend". It is a wholesome story and very impactful, as it is clear how tangible the story is.

Mahtab

I really appreciated the story. I am glad to hear (but not at all surprised) that your stories are moving so many people to tears. The emotion comes through very strongly in your writing!

Mahtab

I enjoyed reading, "Defeat". I very much liked the line wondering if we are characters from a fictional story that's brought to life.

    Mahtab

➢ <u>Dina Kamil</u> (Mahtab's friend)

Hi Mahtab,

Thank you for sharing *Life's Invisible Battles*. I cried at the very first story about writer's mother giving him the name Tohon. I felt like I was intruding because it was such an intimate and personal story. The last line about two souls being united eternally was very powerful.

    Dina

Follow-up note from Mahtab:

Hi *Abbu*,

I am glad that it means a lot to you. I thought it would, and I also think that it is a great achievement to have someone unrelated, whom you have never met, connect so personally and strongly to a story you have written.

    Mahtab

Hi Mahtab,

This is Dina again. I also loved the story on the Boston marathon bomber – "The Foot Soldier".

I really appreciated Tohon's holistic view on it. Because it is true, we always tend to have one-sided snap opinions of people who commit dreadful acts. We do not think about what was going through their mind, like how they are responding to their own trauma. I very much identify with how sensitive Tohon is, always thinking about what the people around that person must be going through, like their mother and father. Your dad must be more sensitive than I am.

Dina

> Sohana Manzoor (Dew)

Dear Friend,

Life is too vast and often appears meaningless, yet these stories bring out meaning even from seemingly insignificant events.

Why and how do you see and write things you write?

Dew

I enjoyed reading "Quest for Truth". One aspect about your writing that amazes me is that you notice the smallest details around you, for example, termites and *babui pakhi*.

Your world view is thought provoking. However, as I have said before, your writing is often quite philosophic and abstract and hence general readers may not always appreciate the content.

Dew

➢ Erphan Shehabul Matin

Dear Tuhin *bhai*,

Many thanks for sharing *Life's Invisible Battles*. The memoir is excellent. You have covered many dimensions of life very beautifully. I really enjoyed reading it. Please keep writing, and I appreciate your sharing.

Shehab

Many thanks for your email. The more I read your notes, write-ups and discussions, the more I discover your deeper side. It is great and amazing.

Yes, your recent visit to Dhaka has brought us close to each other by sharing our thoughts, and we have developed a strong friendship and bond. I am very much grateful to Allah that he has sent you as my brother-in-law.

Shehab

Your story of *Emil Joseph Burcik* has been a great one. Although you had already told me the story in Dhaka, I really loved reading the full story. I read Part-III twice.

Shehab

➢ Saima Matin

Dear *Fupa*,

You are a gifted writer. Your thoughts brought me to tears. So heartfelt, so apt.

Thank you for sharing it with me. I feel very blessed to have you in our family.

Saima

I finished reading *The Jihadi* last night, and if I have to put my thoughts in one word, it would be "overwhelming".

I feel blessed to have known you under different lights, many of which resemble mine. I was most intrigued by the evening at your professor's house. I felt the same comfort and awkwardness as a newcomer. Also, the grad life moments made me realize how common some things were, even years later.

I was fascinated to learn about your experience performing Hajj. I will be honest: I have heard many of our kin describing how amazing it felt during Hajj and Umrah, but it never made me feel like really going for it. Your storytelling skill did that. While I was going through those pages, I said to myself, *how wonderful it would be to actually go there someday*!

Also, the most amazing find for me was to your compassion in practice; how you have given respect to creation other than humans is something I would like to carry forward. It is easy to be selfish, but it is very difficult to practice kindness. You have certainly passed the Bolai's lens on to me!

I wish I could write my thoughts after every chapter, but I am falling short of words.

I loved how the tiniest or even seemingly most insignificant incidents can leave such huge impressions. Be it "The Fakir", "The Uninvited Guest" or "The Invisible World". Most of the chapters left me with some meaningful insights.

One of my favourites from your book was how you felt indebted to the land of your ancestors and the land of your dreams. The American dream, as they say and preach. I have learnt how apt that journey has been for you.

Finally, I believe an author's success lies in the readers' connections with his penned emotions. You have done that brilliantly. At one point, I was not aware that I knew the author personally. I laughed and cried along with your characters. It felt like both fiction and reality all at once.

Thank you, *Fupa*, for *The Jihadi*. I can't wait to see what *Life's Invisible Battles* would unveil.

I am always moved by your thoughts and writing skills. Your wonderful choice of words for how you feel is something that comes very naturally to a gifted person.

If anything, I have learnt to value each chapter of my life more gracefully from your writing.

Saima

I read your story twice and just didn't want it to finish. The way you have addressed such personal stories with great empathy and life experiences is surreal. It makes me look back on my own journey and connect with many lost memories.

Saima

I just read "Quest for Truth". I think the most beautiful thing about your writing is while reading, at some point, I tend to forget the writer is known to me. I am not sure if I am making sense, but the devastating incidents at the end made me teary and helpless at the same time. Reminding how fragile life is, yet not very short for everyone.

I often question myself of our religious beliefs too. I do not blame anyone but the way we were introduced to Qur'an was that it is necessary to be able to recite it in Arabic. It did not matter if one understood the meaning or not. The *Hujur apu* would come, made us read a few pages and it would continue till we were done. What punishments are waiting for us if we do not obey the rules as per Islam were more prominent than what benefits we might acquire.

Attending Holy Cross School in Dhaka was a blessing as I had friends and teachers from all religions. It has introduced me to so many different perspectives. Yet today, at several cases, there is a notion of proving why Islam is superior than the rest.

Your quest is not only yours as it is initiating me to question many aspects of my life, too.

For the dreams you have mentioned – while I was expecting, I once saw my beloved *nanu* and felt the actual warmth of her hand. It might look like a small incident but it made realize Allah must have granted my wish as I was secretly weeping to meet her one more time.

I wonder about a lot of what ifs but also believe in Allah's will. One of my classmates lost her husband during the early months of her marriage in a training helicopter crash. Years later, when she remarried, she wrote about her first miscarriage. Although, we know, Allah does not burden a soul beyond it can bear. How much one can bear, is my question!

As we are aging, I fear the loss of my parents and dear ones. It sometimes keeps me dreaded thinking how I will survive. Being Safeer's mummy, it terrifies me to think how he will survive if I am no longer there. Yet, I feel helpless of being ignorant of the future.

Thank you for sharing so many thoughtful phases of your life, *Fupa*. Each of our journey is separate yet so similar. I pray that you find solace knowing that you are a good man and like any other good man – there are limitations of how much you can do for others. There is said to be another world, and your friends are the luckiest to watch from there – how preciously you have connected to their children.

Saima

> Farzana Matin (Moon)

Dear *Fupa,*

There were many parts in the first half of *Emil Joseph Burcik* that I reread for the beautiful descriptions. But the part where you described getting married in a short span was really interesting to me, as it felt like I time-travelled and was able to see your and *fupi*'s life unfold at a younger age. I also loved how you described the afternoons you spent at your professor's house enjoying each other's company. I cannot imagine how wonderful it must have been having such a supportive mentor.

As you know, *Abbu* has been depressed for almost a year now, so I took the initiative to read him a chapter of your book every day. But the book is so interesting that I finished almost half of it in a day. I noticed how every time I asked *Abbu* about the specific details of the book, he always answered correctly.

Thanks to you for this book has become a source of our bonding experience, which is why I am resisting reading it alone. I cannot wait to finish and share my thoughts with you! Thank you, *Fupa,* for writing this book and sharing it with us. Moon

----

I have finished reading *Emil Joseph Burcik* this morning, and I am still in awe of the emotions I felt while reading it.

As I was reading the book, I interestingly remembered some of the events – for instance, your visit to Washington, DC and our subsequent meeting at New York. Little did I know there were so many personal and professional triumphs, injuries, and life-changing events that led up to that trip. I heard so many stories about your time in Saudi Arabia and Australia, but I knew little about the way the US had impacted your life and professional career. I felt especially connected whenever you mentioned your time at Penn State and UT Austin because I am currently applying for a Master's and often come across those universities in my research.

Your book gave me perspective on how short life is. The way you built such a strong bond with your mentor and continued to keep that relationship not only with him but also his relatives for many generations is a true example of how the family is not always connected by blood. I was crying while reading the letters from Mrs Burcik and the way you kept writing to her at her old address, despite receiving no response. It seems to me you were a son they always wanted. May Mrs. Schwartz and Mr. and Mrs. Burcik rest in peace.

The youngest of the Dr. Burcik's two great-grandsons, Evan, having such a close connection with you was not surprising to me at all because your calm and loving demeanour was the main reason Saima *apu*, Sara *apu,* and especially myself were so fond of you growing up and still are now.

It was heart-warming to see that even though you were never able to convey to your mentor that you dedicated your dissertation to him or connect with him in the same way during his last years, your admiration for him was apparent generations later to his grandchildren and their parents. This was life's way of showing that your love for him was returned even after his soul had departed, and that gives me a lot of hope.

I am very happy you chose to write these memoirs, as I hope Shehraan and Safeer will read your and *fupi'*s books one day and feel pride, astonishment, and inspiration, as I have. I will definitely read the stories you sent me and share my thoughts.

Moon

"Quest for Truth".

I apologize for the late response, and thank you as always for sharing your stories with me. I wanted to make sure I take time out for myself to enjoy this story.

I feel honored to have read these stories and seeing your perspective as you experienced these life events. I read half of the story and immediately sent it to my friends who have asked me previously to share with them your past and present writings.

On my end, I was so pleased to see how you connected the real world to justify God's creations. In order to build an internal connection with God for myself, I have also tried to see His presence in day-to-day life. I would be lying if I said I am consistently grateful for everything I have been blessed with, but I am trying to change that.

In your epilogue, where you mentioned the loved ones you lost, you made me realize how precious every day with your loved ones truly is. I will pray for them to be granted in heaven, but I will also pray that you forgive yourself, as you did so much for those whom you cared for and their families. I truly believe that you are hard on yourself because of the goodness in you, and since a part of God is within us all, He will be so much kinder to you.

Lots of love,
Moon

➤ Rasika Swaminathan (Farzana's friend)
Hi Farzana,

Thank you for sharing with me "Quest for Truth". I am mesmerized as to how many lives the author has lived in one lifetime.

Rasika

➤ <u>Mohammad Quayum</u>

Dear Kabir *bhai*,

I have read your story "Bolai". I found it very engaging and moving. You have done a wonderful job with Tagore's original story. Bravo!

You have turned out to be an excellent writer in English, Kabir *bhai*. Please continue pursuing your passion, and I would like to read more of your stories in future.

Quayum

It is a pleasure to hear from you. Thank you for the update. It is a delight to know that your new memoir has come out. Congratulations! I look forward to reading it. You have really grown as a writer.

I enjoyed reading your journals some thirty years ago, but I was ecstatic to read your rewriting of Rabindranath's short story. It shows you not only have the ideas, but have also mastered the technique of writing. Fantastic! I will look forward to reading more of your work in future.

Quayum

I have just finished reading *Emil Joseph Burcik*. It is indeed a very moving story. I am about to behave like Evan (the best episode in the story), but I am trying to restrain myself.

It reads very nicely; it is very fluid, and the artistic touches are also there. You seem to have mastered the epistolary style of writing. I saw that in "Bolai" and now in this story. Excellent. Please keep writing!

Quayum

I have read your piece "Quest for Truth" with great interest, Kabir *bhai*, and found it insightful and fascinating. It is also nicely written/woven with good images and metaphors. However, I believe it is still incomplete, and that there is more to come. You have not yet told us what attracted the Sufis to the Qur'an. I look forward to the next segment.

Quayum

➤ Khondker Rahman (Babu)
Dear Kabir *bhai*,

It is exactly forty days since I received your last email asking me my opinion on *Life's Invisible Battles*.

Firstly, my sincere apologies that I could not respond to you earlier. Secondly, having had the book in my hand for more than two-and-a-half months, I did not get the chance to open it until last week.

Without defending myself, please know that I am going through the hardest ordeal of my life right now – something I would have loved to share over a coffee with a beautiful soul like yourself. Unfortunately, we have travelled along different paths since we last met, and as it stands, it would perhaps be a dream to meet you in person anytime soon. Hence, my ordeal stays with me for the time being.

I have just finished reading the book. I am simply amazed by such powerful writing. I thoroughly enjoyed reading every chapter – so deep and so touching! During our regular encounters while you lived in Chapel Hill, Brisbane, I did notice that you were a very emotional man with thought-provoking questions regarding our lives and the way we lived it, but I could never comprehend what you actually meant. Now I do.

It is wonderful to read the narrative of your beautiful, expressive deep thoughts. It is simply stunning. I enjoyed the chapter "Only Heaven Knows" the most. I also enjoyed the Bolai's letters – so vivid and intense. I almost travelled back to where you were at that time.

When I finished reading, I felt that the last chapter could possibly have appeared a couple of chapters earlier.

All in all, I cannot thank you enough for sharing your book. I am honoured to know you, Kabir *bhai*.

You have inspired me immensely to write my own story. However, I do not have wonderful writing skills like yours, so I would struggle – but I have a goal to do it one day.

Babu

➢ Mushfiq Rahman

Dear Kabir,

Just to give you a heads up, I have started reading *Life's Invisible Battles*. The first episode clarifies why and how you were named Tohon. I always thought it was a pseudonym! I had already read "The Tormented Soul" when it was first published in the Dhaka Daily Star.

I was moved to tears by your story of Masud, your lost friend. In my mind, even before I came to the end of the story, I already knew that Masud's rocket project would end in tragedy. What brought me to tears was the story of the eighth child of Jishan's *nanu*, with its poignant and uplifting message of quintessential humanity.

Mushfiq

I am happy to tell you I have finished reading *Life's Invisible Battles*. Although only a slim 109 pages, it is dense in content and hence required a lot more time to read and digest compared to a novel of similar length. Besides, there were numerous interruptions, chiefly the American political circus to which I have been glued since the election in November 2020.

I can divide your book into two distinct parts, although they are perhaps connected by a common philosophical underpinning of *life's invisible battles*.

The first half was an easy and smooth reading of some selected stories of your life. You began quite appropriately with *The Battle with Truth* that set the philosophical framework of your book that explores the fuzzy boundaries between truth and falsehood and good and evil. The stories of Masud and Mirzaad are expositions of our quintessential humanity. The story of your "The Foot Soldier" reminded me of Bangladeshi-American Raisuddin Bhuiyan's campaign to save the life of a man who tried to kill him in the aftermath of 9/11. Listen to this great TED talk by second-generation American Anand Giridharadas: *A Tale of Two Americas*.

I had read your story "The Cleaner" when it was first appeared in the Dhaka Daily Star. That story is in keeping with your quest for self-discovery. Being a crime suspect allowed you to articulate your inner conflicts. I am not sure whether the account of the interview with the inspector is a verbatim reproduction of actual transcripts or if you used it as a backdrop to convey your inner battles. In any case, you are within an author's prerogative to reconstruct an event that best highlights the main theme, even if it is not an exact replica of events (in this case, the transcript of the interview – I assume you did not have a recorder with you).

From the halfway mark, the book turns to deeper philosophical territory. Your monologues are thought-provoking. Your series of soliloquies conveys the currents of inner torment that flow in your mind. You have searched for an answer to the many contradictions and seeming absurdities of life through the prism of evolutionary biology. Some of the answers you have found remain to be validated, and I am sceptical about the sweeping presence of embedded memory in our DNA. I myself have had no epiphany about life in a different form in a different era, but that may be just my insufficient depth of perception. I have no proof to disprove your conjectures, and conjectures by definition remain conjectures until proven otherwise through a set of repeatable scientific experiments and observations. Nevertheless, you have presented your readers with some really interesting food for thought, and I commend you for putting your thoughts into words that allow further discussion of the subjects you have raised. It is possible there will be no consensus because humanity has been grappling with these issues since the beginning of time, but at the very least, we will be more enlightened human beings. So, thank you for your book.

Mushfiq

I spent a leisurely afternoon reading and enjoying *Emil Joseph Burcik*. I did something unusual – I read the book in one go. True, it's not a massive book, but my attention span is rather short these days, and I hardly read more than 10-15 pages at a time. However, your narrative kept me going. Each page seemed to hold out the promise of further discovery of convergences of characters, places, and events in the successive pages. I could not put the book down until I finished it.

Your story is both uplifting and sad simultaneously.

It is uplifting to read about your tight embrace of two American families and how they accepted you as one of their own. Love, friendship, warmth and kindness fused together to generate lasting chemistry with many characters, primarily the Burciks and the Schwartzes. The twists and turns of life took you to many corners of the world. However, an invisible emotional chord somehow kept you connected to these people. They were part of your inner sanctum who kept visiting you in your moments of introspection. They were as much your family as your biological family. Reconnecting with the Burcik family was an extraordinary and amazing coincidence. There are far too many cases of lost friends never to be found again.

A search for these kindred spirits is often futile, rekindling wistful memories and generating a trail of silent tears. Fortunately, the trajectories of Tohon (author), Amazon (book seller), and a curious grandson intersected serendipitously to set in motion a deserving reunion amongst the families. The senior Burciks and Schwartzes could not physically participate in this reunion, but their spirits hovered above and their presence was strongly felt. Likewise, each page of this book bears the imprint of their spirits.

The book is also sad because readers can sense and identify with the underlying sense of rootlessness in the human journey. Nothing is permanent. No roots are strong enough to anchor us permanently in our familiar comfort zones. No sooner do we feel settled than the currents and eddies set us adrift again. Nothing seems to be permanent, like a flower after a full blossom, now withered and shrivelled; a sudden gust of wind can blow it away. For humans, all that remains are memories frozen in our minds until those too are washed away by the inconvenience of mortality.

Thank you for presenting this bittersweet memoir. It gave me much joy and food for much thought.

Mushfiq

In an earlier mail on the topic of your book *Emil Joseph Burcik*, I meant to comment on the title of your friend Turgay Ertekin's memoirs – *One Can't Clap with One*

Hand. Perhaps he used a Turkish proverb for the title of his memoir. In fact, we have exactly the same proverb in Bengali - এক হাতে তালি বাজে না. What I wanted to mention is how your book also resonates with the same theme. The love and warmth you received from your American families (the Burciks and the Schwartzes) were matched by your love and affection for them. Such a sublime display of humanity cannot be sustained over a long period of time unless the relationships are underpinned by reciprocity.

Mushfiq

I enjoyed reading your niece, Farzana's feedback and comparing notes. Clearly, there are parts I cannot relate to, like her remembering your visit to New York. But, by and large, there is a great deal of similarity of emotions felt by us both, and that is a mark of success for a writer in triggering similar reactions across his readership young and old.

So, congratulations to you on writing a wonderful memoir spanning several decades of your life that displayed the full spectrum of joy, love, triumphs, and tragedies. The fact that you could distil everything down into a very compact book, short in pages but deep enough to capture all the multifaceted currents of your eventful life, is a great achievement.

Mushfiq

Thank you for sharing your story, "Defeat". I had set aside your write-up to give myself ample time. The title of the piece indicated it was going to be a dense philosophical soliloquy, and to do it justice, I would have to read it slowly.

I commend you for baring your soul and sharing with your readers your inner pain. On the surface, such an internal struggle by a person who ticks all the boxes that define success in life appears counterintuitive.

You have actually found the answer to your anguish, even though your soul has not been pacified by your rationale when you conclude very correctly: *I begin to see that living is rooted in violence, for life is sustained by life.* That statement captures the essence of the ecosystem in which all animals and plants live, thrive, and die. There is no escape from the cycle of life sustained by the food pyramid that has evolved over millions of years. Fortunately or unfortunately, humans sit at the top of the pyramid, but the violence we commit against animals is not an exclusive human monopoly. Predators at one level are prey at another. When a bird eats a worm, the worm is the prey and the bird is the predator. But the worm is also a predator, as it eats microbes, both dead and alive. We do not know whether birds feel the pain of the worm as it swoops on their prey. We assume their brains are not sufficiently developed to undertake complex and abstract thought processes, but that is at best a conjecture on our part.

I found your mention of Cain killing Abel somewhat intriguing. I am not sure whether you mention this in a metaphorical context, or on the basis of acceptance of what is claimed in Islamic, Christian, and Jewish scriptures – not that it matters when it comes to your inner pain. I am not sure whether even unquestioned submission to a religion provides an escape route for coming to terms with what torments your heart and resolving your underlying conflicts.

While I have no means of minimising your inner pain, I think you are a little too hard on yourself. You must not be ashamed of yourself for failing to stand up for your friend Abul Bashar, as you were hardly ten years old. You were still a child. The military cantonments in which you grew up were patterned on command-and-control structures that spawned a certain level of authoritarianism and paternalism. Bullying was a by-product of such cultures! A ten-year-old boy is not sufficiently mature to make conscious decisions. His actions are mostly reflexive, depending on how the brain developed up to that point. Another ten-year-old boy could possibly have acted differently, but not because he was intrinsically more righteous or courageous - he would be acting instinctively. One cannot be too triumphant about an impulsive bold decision, and by the same token, one cannot be too embarrassed by what seems like a timid decision to stay away from a fight. You had no control over your DNA, and sufficient time had not passed to enable your intellect to overcome your instinct.

Finally, I do not understand why this should be your "last and concluding story". Surely, you have many more stories to tell. Please do not stop.

Mushfiq

Thank you for sharing your story, "Quest for Truth", which was deeply engrossing. Your lifelong quest to understand and discover how all forms of life, including humans, fit into the infinitely large cosmic ecosystem is very engaging. Your readers will appreciate your honesty, integrity, and tenacity in probing into the philosophical and spiritual dimensions of our brief and puny lives.

Mushfiq

➤ Jan Willem Roosch
Dear Mohammad,

I have acquired your book *Emil Joseph Burcik*, reading it and enjoying the privilege of being a small part of your world, to learn of your wise views on life and to walk some small distance with you on your exceptional life journey!

After reading the book, it strikes me that you have raised a kind of "literary monument" in honour of your mentor and friend. I found it fascinating, inspiring, and, above all, moving.

Congratulations on your new story that so nicely illustrates many aspects of being human and how cultural divides can be bridged, and also how Time so relentlessly drags everything and everybody along in only one direction.

I notice that you have recognised yourself more as a philosopher (a lover of wisdom) than an engineer, but being multi-talented as you are, this has still made it possible that you and Burcik started to travel together for some time back in 1976. He changed you, and you changed him.

Jan

"Defeat" is a good read. I felt invited to reflect on my own life, my own attitudes towards our fellow animal species, our inability to know what it is like to be a chimpanzee, a dog, a pig, etc. We are beginning to understand the nature of human consciousness, from which we may increase our understanding of animal consciousness.

I am depressed about all the unnecessary violence in the world, the Ukrainian war in particular.

Jan

Many thanks for sharing this story about your "life-long quest", how you were inspired by a variety of religions and at the same time developed your knowledge of and admiration for the world of science and (the laws of) nature. I notice in this personal testimony as well as in your earlier writings a very strong conviction that you are guided by/subjected to a benevolent "God" who intervenes in your and other people's life. I really admire you for the way you have made sense of the development of your inner world, although I do not see any evidence of a genetic basis for any specific religious conviction. You were in a unique position to be exposed to the great religions of the present world at an early age.

I took your story as an inspiration to reflect on my own experience and make a few notes:

In my case there was the story telling at Sunday school of my childhood, where kids age 6-11 were exposed to the nicer side of Jesus as supposedly written up by his friends and forming part of the Bible. As a kid I was prepared to believe in a powerful (omnipotent!) but invisible good father figure who would take care of me and my kin. I thought that was absolutely brilliant and never questioned this concept in the face of all the wrongs and unpleasantness in the world. Then came the moment that I was expected to commit as a young adult (age 17) to the faith of my parents. During preparations I was instructed by the minister of our church (vicar), nice man, great theologist. We had lively debates about the writings in the Bible, where I found many improbabilities, contradictions and outright cruelties. I had by that time already been exposed to secular views of the world to the extent that I could not publicly commit to this faith and in the end, I begged to differ on my sources of ethical thought, good and evil and at that moment took the road towards a more humanistic/utilitarian view of the basics for moral choices. There was no hard feeling on the side of my vicar. As I grew older, I also adopted the scientific method as the only way to "true knowledge". Such knowledge remains conditional as new information may prove it false. Yes, the more we know, the more we find that we do not know. The way I have summarised my own life-long, ongoing quest is probably grossly over-simplified, as it took a long time and much study before I could rule out with "reasonable certainty" the existence of any supernatural gods. But that is where I am now. However, I am a great fan of the "Book of Nature" and the study of nature and of the nature of human thought and consciousness. How Homo sapiens represents the phenomenon whereby the Universe became conscious of itself (ref. Brian Cox). I am absolutely fascinated by the presentations of Brian Cox (Universe being one of his latest BBC series). I was happy to see that we share our admiration for Dawkins' "Ancestors' Tale", but I am unable to see any evidence of a "watchmaker" working towards the fulfilment of a plan.

One contemporary philosopher (Richard Rorty) in his book Contingency, Irony and Solidarity (1989) had opined that our personalities and convictions are very strongly influenced by a number of key persons that we meet in our life. I can see that for both of us.... This kind of "wisdom" I get from my philosophy courses that I follow one evening per month.

Perhaps I can interest you for an old TED Talk by Anil Seth on the nature of human consciousness:

Your brain hallucinates your conscious reality (Anil Seth TED2017)
https://www.ted.com/talks/anil_seth_your_brain_hallucinates_your_conscious_reality?utm_source=tedcomshare&utm_medium=email&utm_campaign=tedspread

Warmest regards,

Jan Willem

➢ Tanni Saha

Dear Tohon,

I like the piece a lot. I have found you more open. You seem to have a sensible mind that interprets life from various angles. In fact, your choice of words amazes me. I wish I could write like you.

Tanni

➤ Late Robert Schechter

Sadly, I have lost Dr Schechter's note on *The Landscape of a Mind*. It hurts me twice. First, I lost him and then, to make things worse, I lost his note – the very last one.

During my visit in 2011, nearly three decades after leaving UT Austin, I found Dr. Schechter in a wheelchair with his vision impaired. He asked me to come closer so that he could feel my face with his two bare hands. He was the only person other than my mother to caress my face to see it.

I may doubt the existence of the world we live in and even the existence of the universe that surrounds us but I have no doubt about Schechter's affection for me.

Tohon

➤ Kazi Shakil (Joi)

Joi,

I am sorry, I have lost your note on *The Jihadi*. I remember our passionate discussion at your house during one of my visits to Dhaka. You are one of the few to pass on the book to your wife, Tahiya *bhabi*. And then, you did something unusual – you bought several copies of the book and distributed them among your friends. I am most honoured and humbled.

Tuhin

➢ Sheila Stanley
Hello Mohammad,

Thank you for sharing your story, "Defeat". You have such a gift of compassion, like my daughter Rachel. Even with your flaws (we all have got regrets; I certainly do), you are a wonderful blessing to people every day because you care about them.

Why would this story be your last story?

Sheila

I loved your heart in your story, "Quest for Truth", remembering your friends and how they have impacted you. I have found Jesus feels our tragedies and disappointments even more strongly than we do and is worthy of being trusted with them. Thank you for letting me share my heart as well!

Sheila

➢ Mark Sykes
The Jihadi
The first thing that struck the reader – and everyone must know that a novel, or any creative writing, takes every reader differently – is the accuracy, the truth of the narrative and the authorial voice. This personal story has creative authority. I appreciate that this imaginative narrative must be based on real events; much fiction has its roots in reality, and it is a direct interpretation of personal experience.

This book could almost be either documentary or fiction. This narrator's description is a situation we have imagined, or met – or at least often seen in passing; but this book brings the reality home. It does not take away from the artistic truth of the book; it is a very effectively presented chunk of relatively real life that speaks with authenticity, in the narrator's voice, and also in the voices of other participants, Emil Burcik in particular.

This is a story of overcoming, a theme which could appear hackneyed were it not redeemed by the characters of the narrator, that hold the narrative together. It is a personal drama that succeeds in communication.

Tohon takes the reader into a powerfully real world of the author's devising. The tone is intimate and conversational, and, as I have mentioned above, it has the strong voice of personal authentic experience.

All writing can be considered as more or less autobiographical, whether it draws on actual or imagined experience because it is from personal experience and observation that the writer creates a world of the imagination.

Tohon gives himself the space to explore and develop the theme – and, finally, to bring us, the readers, to a closure that, we feel, gives a chance for a brighter tomorrow.

Mark Sykes

The Landscape of a Mind
This book is a lively, readable presentation, very generally addressed, of the only question that, ironically, can never be answered, or certainly cannot be given one answer to fit all - WHY?

Tohon does not take up a polemical stance. He is a humanist. He examines the universality of message, and he gives the reader a clear way through some of the chronological and intellectual history of ethical thought. He raises some central matters which may not be common thoughts, although they should be.

One of the qualities of this book is that it may start the casual reader to think less casually. It is extremely easy to read. The author gives the reader a lot of jumping-off points, some of them provocative: OK, he seems to be saying, you don't agree? Right, off you go, read it up, find out for yourself, make up your own mind.

Someone who picks up this book could easily find themselves next reading Darwin, the Upanishads, Bertrand Russell, the Qur'an or Spinoza. This has to be valuable. I have a bad habit of reading three books at once. While I was reading this one, I was also reading Wittgenstein's Tractatus (flawed but fascinating) and the letters of Carl Jung (too many of them), and they were not bad book shelf fellows.

The Landscape of a Mind may appear

simple, but it is certainly not simplistic. An insoluble intellectual problem is made no easier by being dressed up in jargon. Tohon is a profoundly spiritual writer who communicates with his reader in the language of truth and perception.

This is an interesting and, above all, thought provoking book. It has been a privilege to have read it. It presents a poetic distillation of much thought and wisdom in a frame that is not only contemporary but also timeless.

Although it is not specifically theist, it calls to mind a well-known verse from the Qur'an, "*For the man who takes one step towards Allah, Allah takes ten steps towards that man*".

Mark Sykes

Epilogue

As I go through the timeless sketches, waves of emotion overwhelm me, making me cry. So, we now have a situation here – portraits of a bunch of crying painters and a crying sitter. They all look like mirror images of each other.

It has been my lifelong quest to see the invisible mirror. I am now so close, oh God, and yet I miss the mirror.

Acknowledgements

I am indebted to Anis, Amit, Nafisa and Murshed for sharing their personal stories with me and allowing me to publish their accounts.

I have taken the liberty of reproducing my readers' ruminations. I am forever grateful to them all.

I am thankful to Isabel Williams and Robert Fuglei for their editing services.

Lightning Source UK Ltd.
Milton Keynes UK
UKHW040735211122
412554UK00006BB/473

9 781803 695679